Angels of Flesh,
Angels of Silence

BOOKS BY LORNA CROZIER

Inside Is the Sky   *1976*
Crow's Black Joy   *1979*
Humans and Other Beasts   *1980*
No Longer Two People (with Patrick Lane)   *1981*
The Weather   *1983*
The Garden Going On Without Us   *1985*
Angels of Flesh, Angels of Silence   *1988*

Angels of Flesh, Angels of Silence

poems by

Lorna Crozier

M&S

Canadian Cataloguing in Publication Data

Crozier, Lorna, 1948-
Angels of flesh, angels of silence

Poems.
ISBN 0-7710-2476-2

I. Title.

PS8555.R72A84 1988   C811'.54   C88-095059-5
PR9199.3.C769A84 1988

The Publisher would like to thank the Ontario Arts Council for its assistance.

Set in Aldus by The Typeworks, Vancouver

Printed and bound in Canada

McClelland and Stewart
The Canadian Publishers
481 University Avenue
Toronto, Ontario M5G 2E9

For my mother and father and for Patrick

AN ARGUMENT WITH DARKNESS

The heart is an argument with darkness
Patrick writes in his ghazals.

The day falls into itself
becomes without question the night

as we fall into the space
the other makes, our bodies

debating the end of things,
building these words

out of breath and brevity,
these words that argue time.

CONTENTS

CHILDHOOD LANDSCAPES

13   Fear of Snakes
14   Childhood Landscapes 1
15   Sometimes My Body Leaves Me
16   Childhood Landscapes 2
17   Turning into Flesh
18   Childhood Landscapes 3
19   The Oldest Song
20   White Cat Blues
21   Potato Planters
23   When the Sky Got Sick
24   Twins
29   Fathers, Uncles, Old Friends of the Family
31   Living in the Twentieth Century

SOMETIMES FLYING

35   Seasons
36   Angel of Infinity
38   So This Is Love
39   Quitting Smoking
41   If a Poem Could Walk
42   My Aunt's Ghost
44   Ways of Leaving
45   A Love Poem

47   Mother Tongue
49   Sometimes Flying
51   Hands

ANGELS OF SILENCE

59   Angel of Silence
60   Secrets
62   Chile
63   The Pacific
64   A Woman's Shoe
66   The Colour Blue
67   Nothing Missing
69   That Kind of Heaviness
70   Without Hands
72   The Sky at Twilight

THE PENIS POEMS

75   Overture
76   Poem for Sigmund
77   Penis/Bird
79   Literary Allusions
81   What Women Talk About
82   Osiris
83   Variations
84   Facts
86   Phallic
87   Their Smell
89   Tales for Virgins
92   Ode

DREAMING DOMESTIC

97   The Goldberg Variations
98   Picture: A Window, a Woman, Night
102 Domestic Scene
103 Eggs
105 Dreaming Domestic
107 Flowers and Butterflies
109 Home Town
110 Male Thrust
112 Jameson Irish Whisky
114 Red Sweater
116 Cat, French Class, Grocery List, Etc.
117 Fragments for a Long December

THE INFLUENCE OF AN AVID FISHERMAN ON ORDINARY LIFE

125 The Influence of an Avid Fisherman on Ordinary Life
127 Mother and I, Walking
128 Watching the Whales
130 Spider
131 How Beautiful Thy Feet in Shoes
135 Inside, Looking Out
136 Lines for the Earth
137 Afterwords
139 In Praise of Women
140 A House to Live in
141 How to Stop Missing Your Friend Who Died

ICARUS IN THE SEA

145 Icarus in the Sea

157 A Note on the Text

CHILDHOOD LANDSCAPES

FEAR OF SNAKES

The snake can separate itself
from its shadow, move on ribbons of light,
taste the air, the morning and the evening,
the darkness at the heart of things. I remember
when my fear of snakes left for good,
it fell behind me like an old skin. In Swift Current
the boys found a huge snake and chased me
down the alleys, Larry Moen carrying it like a green torch,
the others yelling, *Drop it down her back,* my terror
of its sliding in the runnel of my spine (Larry,
the one who touched the inside of my legs on the swing,
an older boy we knew we shouldn't get close to
with our little dresses, our soft skin), my brother
saying *Let her go,* and I crouched behind the caraganas,
watched Larry nail the snake to a telephone pole.
It twisted on twin points of light, unable to crawl
out of its pain, its mouth opening, the red
tongue tasting its own terror, I loved it then,
that snake. The boys standing there with their stupid hands
dangling from their wrists, the beautiful green
mouth opening, a terrible dark O
no one could hear.

CHILDHOOD LANDSCAPES 1

The moon above the rose beds
is waiting for the blooms
to rise and consume it.

It lowers its ladders of light,
of spider webs. There's nothing else
to do with its time.

The new shoots of the rosebushes
dream their fleshy blossoms,
push the thought of them

so slowly through the night
like stunned white moths
leaving their chrysalides

meeting the moonlight for the first time.

SOMETIMES MY BODY LEAVES ME

Sometimes my body leaves me,
goes into another room
and locks the door. There

it bangs about
like an angry thief.
What is it looking for?

Then there are its silences
stretched thin and taut
between us, invisible

as a fishing line
falling through layers
and layers of green.

I don't know what it feels,
if it feels anything;
or what it remembers,
if each cell holds a memory.

I don't know what sounds to make
to call it back.

What does it do when it sits alone
without a book or anything
resembling love?

On the merry-go-round at twilight
the children you don't see in the day
are spinning. Holding the bars
they run in circles,
jump on the boards and turn and turn.
If you could see their faces you'd know
you'd seen them before
on the posters in the supermarket,
on the back of milk cartons at the breakfast table.

You don't know what to do
when they show up in your neighbourhood,
you don't want to admit they're there.

In the middle of the playground
where you sit in the afternoons, a book
in your lap, your eyes on your daughters,
your small sons, at twilight
the quiet ones are twirling.

Even the dark that moves
from the trees, the back alleys,
the empty lots between the houses
where your children sleep,
cannot hurt them anymore.

TURNING INTO FLESH

Hidden by trees, not deliberately,
just wanting to be alone, I watch a man
not far below me drive a stoneboat
to a hollow in the earth, heave something heavy,
something the size of a full-grown pig
over the edge. Whatever it is gleams
like an animal without any skin.
He leaves without seeing me and I wonder why
I feel such relief. There's nothing to fear.
It's mid-morning. I can hear a tractor
in the neighbouring field, a magpie,
wind in the dry grass. Part of me
wants to walk down that hill, look
over the edge, see what's there.
Part of me stays in shadow,
watches the magpie fall from the branches,
disturb the swarm of flies that lifts
the shape of whatever it is into the air.

He dug until he hit bone
and hit bone again.
The bones began to talk.
He heard his father's voice,
his mother's. They said
such simple things,
asked how he was sleeping,
if he was warm at night.

He could see where
they'd been broken,
where they'd been eaten by lime.

He cleaned the bones
and built a child.
There was only one arm
that worked, only one leg.
He took it everywhere.
It had to lean on him
to walk. He was its voice,
its ears, its eyes.

This child of broken bones,
of bones eaten by lime,
was born here in your city
on the hill where the eucalyptus grow,
where the dead leave their shadows
among the blue leaves.

THE OLDEST SONG

The hens in the dusty twilight of the chicken coop
sing in strange low voices, not the squawking
we think we know, for that is what they do
when we are near. Weird sisters these, all white
the dance they do while the woman sleeps.
Her own small egg, perhaps her last, travels
the dark to its inland sea. Heads swaying from
side to side, the hens all lift one foot, pause,
before they set it down as if it were the first
time they touched the ground, here only for one night,
so white, they could have fallen from the moon.
The woman sinks into feathers, into her own
dark dreams. That part of her that walks in sleep
and won't remember in the sun's first light
wonders at the voices her body moves toward,
the hens singing their oldest song
while strings of moonstones
grow warm inside them.

WHITE CAT BLUES

The white cat with sapphire eyes
can't be colour blind
must see the world
                        as blue.
Blue horses, blue light spilling
from the window, blue willows,
blue women
carrying bowls of bluish cream.

            How beautiful I feel
all blue — shoulders, feet and hair,
the brilliant air,
blue wind
            touching everything.

Tonight desire
            the distance
between the moon and the white cat
sleeping under the apple tree
            (the apples cold and blue)
will be the precise colour
of the cat's dreams of rain.

POTATO PLANTERS

My father digs the hole
my mother drops the potato in –
she's cut them
so each piece has an eye

I wait till my father
empties his shovel
then stamp the earth
with my bare feet

Always it is May
it is after supper
when my father is home
still in his workboots
with the steel toes
his hands smelling
of machines and oil

Later there will be a moon
round and white
as the new potatoes
my mother boils
with milk and peas

I walk behind them
my feet loving the damp earth
my footprints all over the ground

Even now I see us
moving single file in the fading light
we three the last thing
the eye of the potato sees

WHEN THE SKY GOT SICK

When the sky got sick
the surgeon cut it open
said *My God* and left.

Geese picked up the catgut,
pulled it in and out
across a continent, stitches
dissolving
              into a long blue scar.

How pitiful the sky!
How pale in the hot afternoons!
Stars are burning through its skin,
the thin bones ache.

It needs wings to cool its forehead.
Someone send for its relatives –
the snowy owl, the hawk, the great
blue heron.

Everyone else has walked out on it.
Can't you hear the angels
boarding up their windows
and leaving one by one?

TWINS

1

Mother calling,
calling me in to bed,
her voice impatient.

He and I sit in the dark,
so close
I don't know where
                    I begin
and he stops.

Rain falls on our hair,
on our thin
                transparent hands.

2

Dressed in black my brother
lies in the long grass,
plays a Jew's harp. Crickets
stop   when he hesitates
start again.

In and out of sleep
I ride my brother's song,
he and the crickets
                strumming the air
beneath my window.

3

He never comes out of hiding.
I count to ten,
search all the places I've been
but never find him

though I feel his eyes

watching me
like night animals
                    who burn
briefly in the headlights
and are gone.

4

When I think of him
I am rowing a boat with one oar,
night abandons day, a mushroom
forgets its cap in the cloakroom
of the earth.

When I think of him
a mouth is born without a tongue,
a fox without a tail,
a bird with one broken wing
tries to fly.

5

Do I remember us smiling?
Do I remember him curved
around me like a spoon,
both bending
            in one direction
in the closed room of her belly?

Do I remember his head
shrinking like an apricot in a bowl
until he is blue and wrinkled,
pale phallus a maggot
eating its way to the faulty heart.

6

Once he brought home a bloodhound
that never slept. It lay
between us, watched his face,
whining and licking his hand
when he reached for mine across the dark.

7

This is the story of our birth:

We were in a room with a huge window
staring at the sea,
white curtains sucked in and out
with our breath. Sometimes the water climbed
to the door. Golden minnows leapt from sand
like memories, half darkness, half light.

One morning he painted my name
on a wooden boat and pushed from shore
past the birds turning. He looked back
as I waved from the window
                          then jumped
falling until light no longer broke
across his shoulders. My face breaking
just below the surface of the water.

Everything disappeared, the room, the sea,
the boat drifting. Only the sound of rain
from a far distance, my mother calling,
her voice impatient.

8

Brother, why didn't you follow me
out of the womb
into this other light?

9

Something lost
like the words of a song
you loved as a child, like innocence,
a belief in things.

Even now, something lost.
A memory, half pain. I know
your hand touched mine
in the uterine dark. When my eyes opened,
yours were open. They held me
in their clear blue light.

If I had known mirrors then,
I would have known
it was like looking in a mirror
except you didn't come out
from the other side.

When will you return, flesh of my flesh?
I have a cricket in a matchbox, a bird
with one wing. I have saved a raindrop
from the day of our birth. I have made
a room for you inside me.

This morning a boat drifted back to shore.
Under my name, dear brother, I will write yours
in bright red paint.

FATHERS, UNCLES, OLD FRIENDS OF THE FAMILY

Uncle Peter always told me
to wash my hands before breakfast
because I didn't know where they'd been
in the night   what they'd touched

                 and his hands
lifted me from the paddling pool,
young seal   all wet and giggly,
his farmer's hands
soft in the towel,
my mother's
youngest brother
                  pulling aside
my swimsuit.

Then there's the father
                  of my friend
who did it to her
till she ran away from home.
On his seventieth birthday
she visits with the grandchild
he's never seen
and before she can pour their tea,
he reaches out,
                  grabs her breast,
then cries   says he can't help himself
and she cries too,
what's there to say to him now?

One is always
the best friend of the family.
He makes her a fishing rod
from a bamboo pole
and with hooks   with bait,
rows her to the middle of the lake.
Shh, shh, I won't hurt you
                              shhhh.

Years later
          your flesh crawling,
you try not to turn away
when someone you love lays a hand on you.

Where did he touch you?

          Here   and here,
those places no one ever named.

LIVING IN THE TWENTIETH CENTURY

Someone in the house
shouldn't be there. Someone else
opens and closes his hands,
throws a glass against the wall.
The clock keeps ticking   ticking
as if the air moved
on its own delicate wheels.

Someone in the house
pulls on boots, a yellow slicker.
Another has nowhere to go.
He walks out the door and through the garden.
He won't come back.

        Only one
thanks the cook for supper.
She pinches his initials
on top of the buns
with white, dusty hands.

SOMETIMES FLYING

SEASONS

I wish there were a season for mating
like with grouse or salmon (the Atlantic
kind that survives, adding ring after ring
to its scales).
              One time of year
you wanted it,
drumming or defying gravity,
and for the rest
you just went about your day.
A grouse folded in feathers,
a salmon moving its fine bones downstream.

Or being human, to fall asleep
late in the afternoon in a double bed,
naked or not, the body
busy with its own life, giving up
on love and beauty, words
like *hand, shoulder, inner thigh,*
meaning simply what they say.

ANGEL OF INFINITY

When she first touched the angel
her fingers burned
though the angel was invisible,
so much time and space,
so much light. The second time

the angel took shape
under the apple tree. The cat
watched the wings
                        surprise the air,
each feather so pure and well defined
the woman tried to count them
to keep her mind on something real.

What do you ask of the Angel
of Infinity?
More room for your children, more
time, more time.

The cat seemed undisturbed.
He bunted his head
against the angel's legs
as if this were an ordinary guest
with cats of her own
in whatever house she lived in.

The woman felt comfort in this
and in seeing the wind
that lifted her hair
move the angel's feathers
so the air was filled with rustling
softer than the stir of leaves.

Maybe that was the blessing:
the cat purring in the shadow
of the angel's wings,
the apples on fire
                    in their usual way
in the apple tree

the wind
            touching everything
at the same time

SO THIS IS LOVE

"The real love that follows
early delight and ignorance.
A wonderful sad dance that comes after."
                                     − Jack Gilbert

So this is love, a kind of sad dance
and who's leading? I lie in bed
without you, your side not slept in
and I don't care. It's over one more time
just like it's raining once again,
a cat dies, you get another. Call it
the same name, remember the generalities,
not the specifics of such small deaths.

It makes me smile how we said this
is different, we've never loved before,
not really *loved,* you know. So here I am
again, trying to work up some kind of anger,
trying to find a word that fits what I
no longer feel.

The cat we got two days ago lies on your pillow,
purrs like he's been there all his life.
Perhaps he has, it's hard to tell the difference.
The rain feels like yesterday's, the long silences,
the same old tired dance.

QUITTING SMOKING

The phone says smoke when it rings, the radio says smoke, the TV smokes its own images until they are dead butts at three A.M. Three A.M. and the *dépanneurs* are open just for you. White cartons, blue cartons, silver cartons that mirror your face. Behind the counters, the young men who work the night-shift unwrap the cellophane as lovingly as you undo the buttons of a silk shirt, your fingers burning.

•

Your cat is grey. When he comes in from the muddy lane, his paws leave ashes on the floor. The dirty burner on the stove smokes, the kettle smokes, your first, your last cup of coffee demands a smoke. The snow on the step is a long Vogue paper waiting to be rolled. Above the chimneys stars light up and smoke the whole night through.

•

In Montreal there are stores where you can buy one cigarette. Cars parked outside, idle, exhaust pipes smoking. Women you could fall in love with approach you from the shadows and offer a light. The sound of a match struck on the black ribbon of a matchbox is the sound of a new beginning. In every dark room across the city, the fireflies of cigarettes are dancing, their small bodies burning out.

•

Dawn and the neon cross on the mountain melts in the pale light. Another day. Blindfolded and one last wish. Electric, your fingers ignite everything they touch – the curtains, the rug, the sleeping cat. The air around your body crackles and sparks, your hair a halo of fire.

•

Breathe in, breathe out. Your lungs are animals pacing their cages of bone, eyes burning holes through your chest. The shape of your mouth around an imaginary cigarette is an absence you can taste. Your lips acetylene, desire begins and ends on the tip of your tongue.

•

The grey of morning – smoke from the sun settling on the roofs, the snow, the bare branches of maple trees. Every cell in your body is a mouth, crying to be heard: *O Black Cat; O ageless Sailor, where have you gone? O Craven A, first letter of the alphabet, so beautiful to say, O Cameo . . .*

IF A POEM COULD WALK

It would have paws, not feet,
four of them
to sink into the moss
when humans blunder up the path.

Or hooves, small ones,
leaving half-moons in the sand.
Something to make you stop
                         and wonder
what kind of animal this is,
where it came from, where it's going.

It draws nearest when you are most alone.
You lay red plums on your blanket,
a glass of cool cider, two sugar cubes,

knowing it is tame and wild –
the perfect animal –
knowing it will stop for nothing
as it walks
            with its four new legs
right off the page

MY AUNT'S GHOST

My aunt talks of moving –
there's a ghost in her house,
baking bread almost every night.
A good sign, I'd have thought,
the smell of bread in the kitchen,
but she says the ghost is too familiar.
It sits on the edge of her bed,
tries to hold her in its arms.

It, she calls the ghost
though I think it's female,
baking bread and all. It moved in
when Uncle Rusty died. I don't remember
much of him, just his hair,
red as willow wands
and the story of him riding
a huge sow
right through the kitchen on the farm
when he was a grown man.

"He was lots of fun," my aunt says,
though that's the only story I've ever heard.

I like to think of her
while she lies sleeping, the ghost
stirring the yeast, measuring the flour
with cupped hands
the way my mother does,

mixing it all in a chipped enamel bowl,
the kind you don't see much anymore
like my aunt's memories of another time –

Uncle Rusty and the pig
riding through the fields
toward the house,
the only light
spilling from the window
in the oven door,
the pale dough rising.

WAYS OF LEAVING

What I remember best about Rome
is the middle-aged woman
we saw on the path near
the Baths of Caracalla,
sitting in the rain
with her legs straight out,
one elbow leaning on a suitcase,
a plastic kerchief on her head.
A car stopped and a man
leaned out the window, said something
in Italian. She wouldn't look at him,
just shook her head, *no, no,* the cars
honking behind him and he pulled away.

She looked solid and respectable,
middle-class. I wondered
what kind of life
she was walking out of,
what was worse than these streets,
this pouring rain.

A block past,
we looked back, saw the car again,
the man rolling down his window,
the woman shouting now, *No!*
We smiled at that,
not knowing then we would leave each other
just as absurdly, three years later,
in a different country,
in the rain.

A LOVE POEM

(after Susan Musgrave's "Not a Love Poem")

The beautiful woman in her bath,
her breasts floating on the water
like small boats without a captain,
thinks of cockroaches
                            watching from the wall,
though none are there now.

The woman thinks of cockroaches
drawn to the white,
                the mystery of the page
just before her lover writes
                      the first word
and the word is changed
because suddenly a cockroach
scratches its own invisible text,
              a story within a story,
six times over,
something Calvino would love.

While the woman soaps her belly,
her breasts sail off to a warmer country
where there are no screens
to keep out the night
                  and night sends its muses
through her lover's window. The ones
with a carapace, the ones with wings.

Cockroaches skate on his thoughts
like water spiders,
                    they dip their feet.

What they write is truer than anything
he has ever said to her.
                    Solitary and ancient,
without promise, without grief.
When she touches the pages with wet fingers,
there is the faint smell of grease.

MOTHER TONGUE

The snake's
tongue, the first seducer,
black and forked,
it flicked across the woman's skin
and she'd have done anything,
living as she did with a man
who wouldn't touch her.

It was the snake she wanted
not the apple
though she bit into its hard flesh,
finding the star at the centre.

The snake entered
every orifice
long before Adam,
touching every part of her
inside and out,
                    tasting everything.

That's why we've been taught
to fear them.
It isn't the snake itself,
its sudden green or orange flame,
but what it knows.

The sibilant syllables
                    speaking the flesh,

its whole body a primitive tongue
sliding over us,
spelling itself as it moves,
what it is and what it says
inseparable,
             womb-words,
the secret names that Eve knew

before Adam
lined up all the animals
and carved his cold hard alphabet
beginning with the first
letter
of his own name.

Sometimes when you think I'm sleeping, he says, I'm flying in the air, not dreaming, but there without the need for wings.

> *But what have you left me with? she asks. What am I curled around, whose leg is under mine, whose arm do I stroke with my fingers?*

Oh, that's me too, at least what I leave behind, but really I'm far above you, above Toronto and Montreal, so high I can't see anyone, just the lights of those who cannot sleep, the honeycombs of office towers, and sometimes a barge slipping between the dark of sleep and the other dark of night.

> *But what if the baby gets sick, what if the house is on fire, what if someone breaks down the door and you're not here?*

You and the baby and the house are so small, I could hold you on my fingertips.

> *I'll break your arms, I'll break your fucking legs.*

I'm far above you, darling, where you cannot reach, flying out of your thoughts of me.

> *I never stop thinking of you.*

Oh yes, when you're asleep, when you fall into that part of you where I and the baby, this room, this bed, do not exist.

Are you having fun up there without me?

Remember as a child lying on the grass, looking at the stars till you looked right past them, you made yourself so small you didn't exist in time? Remember how scared you got, how you had to say a name to come back, or turn towards the house, wishing your mother would call you in to bed?

Yes.

Well, that's how it is. Except your mother never calls and you can't say the word that's on your tongue. So sleep, my love, and dream of me, sometimes lying here beside you, sometimes cold and longing for your bed.

HANDS

1

Hands are always travelling.
See the maps on their palms,
forks in the road,
migratory crossings.

When the lights go out
in the neighbourhood,
they go off in the rain
without an umbrella.

They head into a blizzard
with no weather report,
no survival kit.

So what if their shoes
are full of holes,
they don't need them.

In the middle of the night,
blind and naked,
they go their way.

2

Where are they going?
To the place where their lifelines meet.

Will they come back?
If you leave them a skein of wool,
a water basin, a little colour
for their nails when the moon
goes out.

3

While you sleep, your hands
build a city, a house,
a church with a steeple.
Inside there is a funeral.
One hand preaches, the other
lies in a pocket. Inside
there is a wedding.
One holds a ring,
the other weeps in a closed room.
The right never knows
what the left is doing.

4

In each hand
the sound of the sea,
wind in a hollow
skull, the sound of
a thought beginning.

Cup one to your ear.
It will whisper
what the palm says
to the fortune teller,
what the thumb says
to its family of fingers.

5

They turn so easily
into animals, into shadows
of animals dancing on a wall.
There is a hare, a fox
hunting a hare, a cariboo,
its antlers full of singing birds.

The hands themselves are singing.
Listen: each finger is a choirboy
with a red face, his voice
on the verge of changing.

6

The sky is full of hands:
the five fingers
              the points of a star,
each nail glowing with its own light,
its own small moon
that never rises.

7

The left hand is a trickster.
From behind your ear
it plucks coins, roses,
memories of another country,
another age. It is always
night, the windows shuttered.
The hand walks the streets
like a soldier,
broad-shouldered and swaggering,
making you stay inside.
You don't know if this is now
or long ago.

8

The right hand is a changeling.
You find it by your door
in a willow basket.
Its nails are pink.
Someone has scraped away
its fingerprints.
It is as innocent
as anything
you've ever seen.

9

Two hands.
Open   close,
come together.

Closer to the dead,
the living,
          than you.
They cut the birth cord,
they wash the body.

They tie the laces
of your first
          your last
pair of shoes.

10

One hand forms a cock,
the other a vulva.
They bring them together
while you lie sleeping.
One is a devil's, the other
an angel's. From these
two hands are born.
Each knows exactly
what the other is doing.

ANGELS OF SILENCE

ANGEL OF SILENCE

The angel of silence
walks into the room
                (with a sound)
just below
the threshold of your hearing
like snow
        falling while you sleep.

You sense her
            the way a woman knows
something without words
                        whispers from the dark
waters of the womb.

That's the angel of silence
too. The tongues of birds
before dawn, the blue
mouths of horses, their
breath
        rising in the cold air,
your sleep,
and your awakening,
the whole world
                white.

SECRETS

*"From the most remote age, women
have listened to men's secrets."*
— Pablo Neruda

They listened to generals,
to spies, to princes.
They listened to priests
and their stories of the holy trinity,
to poets who named all
the parts of their bodies,
to doctors who named them
differently.

They listened to butchers
with the cries of animals
trapped in their hands,
to bakers who left white whorls
on their breasts and bellies,
to plumbers, to sages, to miners
who wouldn't let them
turn out the light.

They listened to carpenters
with two, sometimes three
fingers missing. They listened to
someone's son, someone's father,
someone's husband. They were known
by the secrets they kept.

They listened to artists
who gave the perfect gift –
an ear.

And when the courts said
A woman has no soul
perhaps the judges
they listened to
thought there was no room for that
a woman packed so full
of what was whispered in the night
she fattened
like a huge termite
that could not move

swollen
with ten thousand secrets
to be hatched
to gnaw through wood
and make a whole
city fall.

CHILE

There's one light
burning in your neighbourhood.
Is it the widow
measuring her hours,
or the baker his flour,
the yeast exploding in sugar water.

In the street
metal calls to metal.
The mongrel barks once,
then is silent
like a mouth stuffed with rags.

You cannot sleep.
A light is burning.
Is it you
who is on the list tonight?

Right now I am the man in the Colville painting
staring at the Pacific. Behind me on a wooden table
that took months to build, dot by dot,
a Browning automatic. For the last time
I am watching a wave as it curls on itself,
rolling over and over. I've lost my breasts,
the curve of my waist and hips. I fit into
my new pants neatly, into my close-cropped
head floating above the painter's panel.
My other body lies somewhere else, perhaps
in a room that begins now. A woman and a dog,
she indistinct, but every hair on the animal
palpably there. Perhaps a mouth begins to open
on her left breast where the bullet
speaks its one clipped syllable. Right now
I am the man looking at the ocean. Inside
the head I've placed above my torso,
one thought turns over and over and won't go
away, the wave curling indifferently a precise
distance from the gun and table, a ruler
carved into its surface, inch by inch,
as if everything were measurable:
death, time, intent.
My new acrylic body about to move.

A WOMAN'S SHOE

They are moving the bones
in Santiago, making way
for the new.
                    The open
graves of the poor are holes
in the earth, utilitarian and simple,
the perfect shape
                    for a body,
nothing more.

Yet in one there is
                    a woman's shoe.
A black high-heel,
a platform sole.

It's a shoe
to stand tall in,
to make her hips swing,
her back arch, her breasts
push against her blouse.
It's the kind of shoe
                    a woman wears
to please a man.

It makes you think
                    of cigarettes and lipstick,
the sound of heels climbing the stairs

after dark, the flare of a match,
a button falling to the floor.

You can feel the leather
on your own foot
                    the weight
on your instep, the high arch.
You wore shoes like that
fifteen years ago.

Fifteen years ago a woman
walked to meet a man.
Her shoes made their own sound
on the ground. She floated
high above them
                    so tall
she knew they could take her anywhere,
even here

where a woman is built
from the ground up –
starting with one shoe,
a black high heel,
an open toe

THE COLOUR BLUE

Distance and desire.
A memory of rain.
A wineglass thrown against the wall.

The colour around a cut
when it begins to heal.

Blue nights when you lose yourself,
when light glints off
so many edges   your skin
growing stars.

NOTHING MISSING

Mother and I wait for my father
who has gone into the labyrinth of rooms
where life and death dance like angels
on the tip of the doctor's tongue.
His cancer's been gone fifteen years
so we relax a bit, flip through magazines.
In the corner on TV young, firm women
bend, stretch, say *Don't stop now!*
There's nothing wrong with those bodies,
nothing missing.

I tell Mom about my friend Mary
who's just lost her breast,
about the purple scar stretching
like a run-on sentence across her chest.
Mom talks about a woman she knows
who lost both years ago
but found the solution to foam falsies
that didn't sway when you walked
or give when you touched them.
Bird seed, she says, *Frieda Yuricks*
uses bird seed stuffed in cotton.
I guess it works real good.

Later after Mom and Dad are on the road home,
the check-up good for another year,
Mary and I laugh over a bottle of wine.
She imagines stuffing her bra with bird seeds,

wonders what she'd do if she went swimming.
Wouldn't the seeds swell?
No need for bust developers here.
From 32 to 42 in fifteen easy minutes.
And what of sprouting?
Green tendrils
crawling up her cleavage.

I imagine Mary sitting in a park
surrounded by sparrows and chickadees,
the brave ones lighting
on her hair, her arms,
her soft, full breasts.

THAT KIND OF HEAVINESS

This morning, a heaviness to everything.
Even the crow is having trouble
lifting the air above its wings. The light
is heavy, the wind in the branches, the
silence between one thought and the next.
It is the feeling that follows
a long afternoon sleep in a strange house,
remember as a child, every object
solid and unfamiliar, holding you there,
alone and not quite human. Watching
the wings of the crow lift and fall,
I think of you, wonder if you sleep
long into the afternoon in another's bed.
I remember your story about the gopher
you shot and shot with a BB gun,
you cold and young, with no regrets.
The gopher pumped so full of pellets
it couldn't run, but dragged its belly
across the grass. That kind of heaviness.
The one the heart knows, its small gut
full of lead.

WITHOUT HANDS

(In memory of Victor Jara, the Chilean musician whose hands were smashed by the military to stop him from playing his guitar and singing for his fellow prisoners in the Santiago stadium. Along with thousands of others, he was tortured and finally killed there in September, 1973.)

All the machines in the world
stop. The textile machines, the paper machines,
the machines in the mines turning stones to fire.
Without hands to touch them, spoons, forks and knives
forget their names and uses, the baby is not bathed,
bread rises on the stove, overflows the bowl.
Without hands, the looms
stop. The music
        stops.
The plums turn sweet and sticky and gather flies.

Without hands
        without those beautiful conjunctions
those translators of skin, bone, hair
two eyes go blind
two pale hounds sniffing ahead and doubling back
to tell us
      of hot and cold or the silk of roses after rain
are lost
      two terns feeling the air in every feather
are shot down.

Without hands my father doesn't plant potatoes
row on row, build a house for wrens,
or carry me
from the car to bed
when I pretend I'm sleeping.
On wash-days my mother doesn't hang clothes
on the line, she doesn't turn the pages of a book
and read out loud,
or teach me how to lace my shoes.

Without hands my small grandmother
doesn't pluck the chicken for our Sunday meal
or every evening, before she goes to sleep,
brush and brush her long white hair.

The sky at twilight is a tender beauty.
We've been travelling, I've been sick,
now we're home again. The first day
I helped you plant the garden,
dug holes for fifty gladioli.
They were the favourites of my grandmother.
Flowers of resurrection:
one wilts, another opens on the long stem,
flowers of dying-in-stages.
Make sure, you said, *they're right side up*
before you cover them.

Last week in another country
I was cold and sick. Desire
left my body, it pulled away
like birds leaving the jacaranda trees,
flying north to our cottonwoods and spring.

Today the bulbs buried in the earth
begin to awaken from their deep sleep.
They have a dumb patience
like our bodies when they are ill,
asexual and tender, twilight
giving way to dark.

A week ago I had to lean on you
to walk. Now we hold one another
in the upstairs room,
the bulbs in the garden,
each turned right side up.

THE PENIS POEMS

OVERTURE

O penis,
apostrophe of lust,
come out of the cage
where you lie sleeping.

O snow leopard,
lithe and rare,
when you raise your head,
the birds tremble in the trees,
are struck
       like wooden matches,
flames falling around you
feather by feather.

O cock of the walk,
O proud rooster who struts his stuff,
come near.
Your comb is carnelian and brilliant,
I want to wear it in my hair,
I want to put it to my lips
and with tongue and tissue
play you
your favourite song.

O prick of delight,
O word made flesh,
I turn out all the lights
so I can hear you.

POEM FOR SIGMUND

It's a funny thing,
a Brontosaurus with a long neck
and pea-sized brain, only room
for one thought and that's
not extinction. It's lucky
its mouth is vertical
and not the other way
or we'd see it
smiling like a Cheshire cat.
(Hard to get in the mood
with that grin in your mind.)
No wonder I feel fond of it,
its simple trust of me
as my hands slide down your belly,
the way it jumps up
like a drawing in a child's pop-up book,
expecting me
to say "Hi!
Surprised to see you,"
expecting tenderness
from these envious woman's hands.

PENIS/BIRD

There's an Indian story
about a boy who desires a girl
he can't have. She sleeps
in innocence, surrounded
by brothers and sisters,
her parents a hair's breath away.

The boy's penis grows wings,
it flies through the smoke hole
and straight to the girl
as if her lap were full
of bread crumbs and berries.

I love that story, the penis with wings
more believable than a swan, somehow.
And here, the girl wanted it,
found pleasure
stroking this strange bird
that came from nowhere,
that sang so sweetly
and nested between her thighs,

the breath of her family
close around her,
warming her naked skin.

I like to think of that bird-penis
winging its way back to the body,

a little worse for wear
like a tattered crow
with some feathers missing,
maybe enjoying flight
more than it should,
the boy anxiously
watching the sky.

D.H. Lawrence described it as
"thick and arching," (the woman's
eyes were reverent). He called it
"lordly" and "the king of glory."
It rose from a "little cloud
of vivid gold-red hair."
"But he's lovely *really*," Lady Chatterly said
although she was startled and afraid.
"A bit terrifying, but lovely. And he comes
to *me*!"

Why, it even had a name –
John Thomas – a double male whammy.

I've never come across a penis with a name,
though I've met one
that could have been called
Humphrey Bogart (it had that kind of
talk-out-of-the-side-of-the-mouth
personality and smelled of smoke).

They're certainly individual things,
some pale with a bluish tinge, others
red as strawberries,
some shy as a sparrow in the hand,
some straight as a surveyor's rod,
others with a bend as if they didn't know
which way they're supposed to go.

You could tell a lot about a man
by the name he'd choose.
Don't bother sneaking a look
at the size of his thumbs
or staring at his nose,
just ask him straight out,
"What do you call your penis?"

A little personal perhaps,
but it's something
you should know. I mean,
what if he named it after his mother?
What if he called it Long John Silver?
What if he called it Moby Dick?

WHAT WOMEN TALK ABOUT

Sure, I'm a woman who likes her pleasure,
but I never understood why the world
turns on it, why life or death
depends on its size. None of my women friends
talks about that,
whether they've bagged a big one
like a poacher in a forest.
They're more likely to talk about
the politics of housecleaning,
if he'll scrub the toilet
or cook a meal. Once on a TV talk show
I heard Germaine Greer, badgered by the host,
say, "Do you think a prick's the most interesting
thing we can put inside us?"
That got me thinking for a long time.

OSIRIS

Isis, a trinity of
mother, sister, lover,
sailed around the known world
and gathered up his parts,
the head, limbs and organs,
Osiris,
pieced together like a broken cup.
All that was missing was his penis.

How different our world would be
if she had left him so.

But she made one out of clay,
rolled it between her palms
the way we roll cookie dough,
sang it to life
between his thighs.

Was she tempted, the clay
wet with her spittle,
to shape it differently,

to make a rose,
a fish, a six-pointed star?

To make an owl,
a crescent moon, a second
pair of eyes,

to carve with a paring knife
another heart.

VARIATIONS

Old man with your teeth
in a glass by the bed,
you're your own crutch
to lean on.
You were born bald
and you've stayed that way,
no toupee will do.

Headless rooster
at the chopping block
you flap about
without beak or brain,
banging
into everything,
bruising the air,
not knowing
when it's time to stop.

Common garden slug,
ugly and beautiful,
your antennae
little horns of light,
on my breasts and belly
you draw a luminous
silver trail
like the moon's
ghostly tracks
across a field of snow.

FACTS

The prick of a cat is
red. It has a bone and barbs.
That's why the female screams.
It tears her inside
when he pulls out.

A drone explodes
when he mates
with the honeybee queen,
his genitals wedge in her waist
like shrapnel.

The penises of some whales
extend over six feet long,
their testicles
weigh half a ton. No wonder
they stay in the sea.

On average a man's
measures five to six inches,
erect. Smooth and boneless,
it has a foreskin
that may have been removed.
Most of the time it is flaccid,
small and harmless
as a plum.

On the surface it seems less

dangerous,
            less dramatic,
in fact,
almost boring. But facts
don't tell us everything.

So much depends
on setting, on intent,
the strange and delicate
anatomy of love.

PHALLIC

Carrots and parsnips,
young red rhubarb shoots
poking through
the soil. An amaryllis bud
just before it opens,
asparagus (mmmm, lightly
steamed, a touch of lemon),
cucumbers, zucchini, some
scarlet runner beans,
green thumb
        alter-egos,
how you tend them,
how you coax them
with your gardener's hands
to make them grow.

THEIR SMELL

Some smell like root cellars,
potatoes and crab-apples
devouring themselves,
turning soft and brown inside. Some
of morel mushrooms in a paper bag,
the smell of earth
under a mound of damp leaves,
rosemary, marigolds, dead roses.

Some smell like geranium leaves,
like burnt stubble
when the smoke's so thick
it changes the light. Others,
the hands of a Chinese cook,
a bale of hay covered with snow,
old-fashioned hair oil. Some
of rancid butter or a fridge
when it goes crazy,
growing its blue, green and black
gardens of mould. Some smell
like anchovies, others balsam poplar,
high-bush cranberries, dusty feathers,
a mouse's nest
in the pocket of an old coat bought at a rummage sale.

Some have a smell
you can't put your finger on,
like the scent of fear other animals pick up

and those high-pitched sounds
we never hear,
                 what our bodies know
but can't put words to,
subliminal,
and most persuasive.

First there's Sylvia Plath's
heroine in *The Bell Jar.*
Her first time,
she bleeds all over the bed,
soaks through the towels
she wears like a diaper,
fills up her shoes
(talk about red
dancing slippers),
then bleeds all over the taxi
that takes her to the hospital –
her mother
out there somewhere,
waiting.

Then there's Ducharme
from the Coast,
hanged for murder,
a penis so big
he rammed it right through a woman
and killed her
though he said he didn't mean to,
all he wanted, your Honour,
was a little love.

Though Protestant,
when I turned thirteen
I dreamed of becoming a nun

wed to Jesus
who never had a penis.
Or even his mother Mary
wouldn't be so bad.
She only had to do it once
and in her ear.

My friends who lost
their virginity
said going all the way wasn't worth it,
especially the ones
who ended up with babies,
folding diapers in front of game shows
while I shook my pom-poms
in the school gym, sex
stale and sweet in the sticky air.

Later in the back seat
it was up to the girl
to say No!
even though she got sick of being
an expert of flying elbows
and crossed knees.

There were all those warnings,
those stories of girls gone bad,
the ones who hung around
the Voyageur Cafe.
Wherever they were going we knew
we didn't want to be.

Better to remain a virgin
to save yourself
like you saved those valentine-
shaped boxes with their dusty ribbons,
their plastic roses. Each of us had
at least one to keep our secrets in –
while we waited for the boy
we couldn't say no to,
though he might hang in the morning,
though we might walk
across our mothers' spotless floors
in bloody shoes.

ODE

To you who are mysterious
and familiar

coddled like a family pet,
a mongrel
born from one who is tame,
another who leaps the fence
then disappears
                    into the hills.

I know you could turn on me
at any moment. Never

trust an animal
that has tasted blood.

•

To you who love the dark,
who dream of the inland sea
and its salty taste.

To you who travel by touch
blind as a bat,
                    finding moths
soft as flannel
in the fragrant night,
the round, ripe fruit.

You have many faces
under your dark hood.

Sweet between my thighs,
you burrow there, the animal
I long for,
the animal I fear.

•

To you who can make yourself
invisible. For years
you have waited
                  for the child,
the solitary woman.

You come in the night
in your soft shoes,
your coat with no pockets.
You batter down the gate,
break the lock,
smash the window.

In my bedroom doorway
you cast the long shadow
of a man.

DREAMING DOMESTIC

THE GOLDBERG VARIATIONS

Never have I felt so unconnected
to everything. Light and its absence.
Rain. The cat on the windowsill catching flies.
Glenn Gould playing the Goldberg Variations
his last time.
        The endless variations of you,
making coffee, ordering seeds for the garden,
calling me upstairs to love. By our bed,
in *Equinox* a photo of an astronaut,
solitary figure
            floating in the cold blue
of space, connected to nothing, touching
nothing. Gould's fingers on ivory keys.
It isn't Bach he's playing
from the grave, the stopped heart.
So free of gravity the mind lifts
like a feathered seed, only
a thin shell of bone holding it in.
Not Bach, but music before it became
the least bit human.
        Is this ecstasy,
this strange remoteness? Rain falling
from such a distance. Gould's Goldberg
Variations. Your hands. The cold
cold blue. My skin.

PICTURE: A WINDOW, A WOMAN, NIGHT

(after reading Patrick Lane's "There Is a Time")

The window hangs
                from the night sky.
Like a figure in a portrait
a woman sits in the centre of its frame,
staring at her hands.
Tonight they are not part of her.

It's not that they belong
to someone else. Tonight
they are simply themselves.

•

The woman is waiting.
A man moves toward her
                from a long way off.
He could be on horseback
or driving a car
           or walking in heavy boots.
Maybe it is snowing
and she is afraid he'll lose himself.

A child calls from another room,
she doesn't hear.
Perhaps no one moves toward the house,
no one calls

from a room you cannot see.
There is only the window,
its square of light,
and a woman waiting.
The sound of her breathing
fills the spaces between her heartbeats
like cotton wool.

•

In summer, the night is short.
She can put it in a box, slide it
under her bed. In winter
night needs a whole house
to live in.
        It is heavy
on the roof like last year's snow.

She could pull on her boots,
climb the ladder
and sweep the shingles,
but she will stay in her chair,

the window measuring
                  the distance between
her face and darkness,
night taking on the shape
of her body,
        the smell
of her long black hair.

•

The moon slides by the window,
light touching one object,
                    then another.
First the table, its white cloth,
then the kettle, the copper
reflecting a face
                the woman should know.

She sees her high forehead,
her pale neck
                but what is in between
is too open, too beautiful

like the face of a blind woman
who doesn't know
someone else is in the room.

•

If the door were to open now,
                it would swing inward this far,
wind slipping in like a cat
brushing her ankles,
then gone.

•

The window is low.
If it were round
the woman would be going somewhere,
drifting through the dark
as if morning were a harbour,

shimmering like heat waves
in the distance,
                    rich with music,
a strange language, a kind of promise.

●

If this is a story about a woman
when you look through her window
you might see her
ironing, her hair in damp curls
on the back of her neck.
                    You might see her
writing, adding up her losses,
knitting something from blue wool.

Tonight she is only sitting in a chair,
hands in her lap.
                    She is imitating
loneliness, practising absence.
If she could choose a title
for this picture, she would call it
nothing.

●

DOMESTIC SCENE

I mop the floors, admire again the grain,
the beautiful simplicity of wood.
The cat we named Nowlan after the poet
who just died, cries for his tin of fish.
You stuff our salmon with wild rice
and watercress, its flesh pink
as Nowlan's mouth, his perfect tongue.
How lucky we are to have found each other,
our fine grey cat, a fresh Atlantic salmon.
Tomorrow we may get drunk and fight
or buy two tickets to Madrid.
But tonight the light in our kitchen
is as good as you'll find anywhere.
The plates glow with possibilities
and the cat licks himself completely clean.

EGGS

Mary won't eat chicken
because she dreamed a hen
with her daughter's head
spoke to her.

She takes this for an omen
and why not? What's more female
than a hen, its rosary of eggs
growing inside, each
a memory of self,
a first genesis, the yolk
spotted with blood –
an image held in our brains
before our birth.

There's something about chickens.
As a child I loved to clean them,
push my hand into the cavity
(like the space I knew
inside me) pull out the guts,
the heart, the gizzard with its stones,
the tiny eggs warm in my palm.

Nothing was like the diagrams
in our health texts in school.
In the kitchen there was shit
if the skin of the intestines broke
and always there was blood.

The blood that made me
bend in pain
was a secret no one talked about.
Then I was the daughter.
                         My head
separate from my body
knew more of a chicken's
than my own.

DREAMING DOMESTIC

Baking is unpropitious for women.
To dream of an apron signifies
a zigzag course. For a school girl
to dream that her apron is loosened or torn
implies bad lessons.

To dream of puddings
denotes small returns from large investments,
if only you would see it.
For a young woman to prepare a pudding
forecasts her lover will be sensual and worldly minded
and if she marries him
she will see her fortune vanish.

If a woman dreams of eating bread
she will be afflicted
                    with children.
Of stubborn will.

To dream of noodles denotes an abnormal
appetite and desire.
There is little good in this dream.

A young woman dreaming of eating pickles
foretells an unambitious career.
If she dreams of basting meats
she will undermine her expectations
by folly and selfishness.

Beans are a bad dream.

To see or eat cooked beef
brings anguish surpassing human aid.
If beets are served in soiled or impure dishes
distressful awakenings will disturb you.

To dream of eating bananas
foretells an uninteresting and unloved companion.
To dream of eating an orange
is singularly bad. For a woman

to dream of making pies
implies she will flirt with men
for a pastime.

She should accept this warning.

A found poem, from Ten Thousand Dreams Interpreted *by Gustavus Hindman Miller, 1931.*

FLOWERS AND BUTTERFLIES

Miriam, an older poet I admire,
takes me aside, tells me
she remembers when I was young
I read a poem about flowers
turning into butterflies
or butterflies becoming flowers,
she can't remember which,
but it stayed with her, that image
or the image in reverse
and she told me then
I'd be good if I kept at it.

I know I'm supposed to say
her words meant a lot to me,
kept me going,
but I don't remember that meeting
or a poem about flowers and butterflies.
It doesn't even sound like me.
Still, she insists,
it's so clear and I was very young.

Maybe it's like the stories
Allen Sapp tells about his paintings,
how he fills you in
on what's happening outside the frame.
(He paints a man on a horse, looking for a cow
and he tells us the man found the cow
out here, where the painting stops.)

Maybe off the page
where my voice couldn't go,
petals open slowly like a poem beginning,
butterflies pause among leaves
to rest their wings
and like it there
where words can't pin them down.

So here it is, Miriam, years later
a poem for you, one you remember,
full of butterflies and flowers,
a still, a moving wing.

HOME TOWN

I like the kid who wrote on his first year
history paper: "The Holy land is sorta like
Christ's Home Town."

He must have been from a town
with a Pool grain elevator, a Chinese cafe,
and one main street no one bothered to name.
One of those places you leave
but want to come back to.
A place where your friends return
for the high school reunion (there were only six
in your graduating class), where you fall in love again
with your grade nine sweetheart and marry her
and it works.

One of those places you dream about
when you're stuck in the city on a muggy day
and the desert you have to cross to get there
keeps growing.

Not that it's perfect,
not that it doesn't have its share of wife-beating,
racism and down-right human greed.
But Christ would've liked the town
this kid's from. Maybe it's even got a name
like *Manyberries, Porcupine Plain,* or *Paradise Hill.*

MALE THRUST

"I can take no pleasure from serious reading ... that
lacks a strong male thrust."
       – Anthony Burgess

This poem bends its knees
and moves its groin.
It does the Dirty Dog
at parties. It pushes
against cloth, against
the page. It pokes
between the lines.
It breathes deeply,
closes its one eye
and wets its lips.
It writes lewd words
in the margins.
Wherever you are reading –
on the bus, at home
in your favourite chair,
in the library –
it flips open its coat
and flashes.
It backs the librarian
against the wall,
it comes
all over the stacks,
over *A Clockwork Orange*,
over *The Naked and the Dead*,

over *A Golden Treasury of Verse*,
over *Sexus, Nexus* and *Plexus*.
This poem won't stop.
Even when you close the book
you can hear it
making obscene sounds,
smacking its lips,
completely in love
with itself.

JAMESON IRISH WHISKY

(for Sean)

John Jameson is the kind of guy
who doesn't know when to go home.
He sits between us at the table,
quiet, shoulders sloped,
a little shy you think at first.
Unobtrusive, he arrives at four,
stays through supper and doesn't leave
when the dishes are put away.

John Jameson fills the room
with smoke. Ashes drift from ashtrays,
turn our faces grey.
He loves old Dylan records,
makes you say *Listen to this cut,*
though no one wants to.
He's a show-off really.
You have to shout when he's around.
Your hands go wild, bruise the air
until the air turns dark.

When you see yourself in his eyes
you look older.
In the back of your neck
pain stretches itself awake. A lean cat
it climbs slowly up your skull
to settle in, knead your brain with grey paws.

We'll not have him back
you say as you turn out the lights
and lock the door.
But the smell of him lingers in your pores
like the smell love leaves
on the sheets and pillows of your bed.

RED SWEATER

You are fishing with your two boys
in a blue canoe. You've paddled past
the dock to the pools
where the jackfish feed. Maybe
a pickerel is moving
                    its huge mouth
to the barbs the boys cast and reel in,
hooks bright as candles
lowered into night.

The wind off the water is cold,
waves slapping the shore with the sound
of hands hitting skin.
                    You've gone so far
I can't see you, only your red sweater
and their lifejackets, there were only two,
and by rights, they're wearing them.

Watchful as a mother on the beach,
I am watching you
                    so you won't disappear,
the canoe tip and you fall in,
your sweater,
your heavy running shoes
swallowed by the waves,
above you the children
floating on the water like peonies

in a blue enamel bowl.
If I had a choice, I'd choose you.

Later they will cast from the pier,
call *Dad* when something tugs on the line.
We'll be lying under sleeping bags
and I'll hold you as you fall
into a different dark, the one your body
calls desire. Now I am watching
your red sweater. Unwinding the wool
and knitting it again.
I add a snail's shell,
a fish scale, the lake's smooth skin.
Fierce as a mother,
I click my needles, I knot the threads,
I pull you in.

The cat rolling on the rug, the poem
begins here, how beautiful his body,
his grey, striped fur. I want to stop
the mind's wandering, the hum of the furnace,
the conjugation of *être* for my French class
tomorrow, the *passé composé*, the *conditionnel*,
the grocery list in the pocket of my jeans,
milk and lemons (your handwriting) *fresh parsley*
if you can find it, grey cat on the rug,
only himself and his body's knowing,
our bodies too, how to stay in them,
the mind in the fingers, the smell of you
on my mouth, *l'article indéfini*, a cat.
Berger's question: What does it mean
when an animal looks at you? That moment
of recognition, that seeing: in Florence
seeing *David* the first time, not still
but only a pause in the movement, the arm
about to rise, the leg follow through, marble
veins warm to the imagined touch, here
and here the blue of your inner thigh
where I place my finger, conjugate
desire, *je suis, tu es, une* and one,
I can't say *un*, my tongue twists
on the vowel, a poem
starts here,
cat rolling on the rug,
parsley for the sweet potatoes,
the poem tongue twister,
paws in the air

FRAGMENTS FOR A LONG DECEMBER

*

In this month of long nights
everything moves inside
                    or moves away;
the shortest day
will be grey and bitter cold
though the snow gives us
                    a kind of light
when the moon hides
and the lights go out
in the neighbourhood.

*

Sparrows churr on the fence,
feathers fluffed like dusters.
The cat paces
            his teeth chattering.
When we let him out, the birds
turn to snow. He looks at us
through the window as though
we have betrayed him
                    dropped him
with a stone in a burlap sack
into the cold
            the empty day.

*

In the supermarket it is still
summer. Butter lettuce. Avocados.
Golden apples with skins of wax.
Oranges we used to call *Japs*
but now are Mandarins.
The trick as a child
to remove the peel in one piece.
                Jap Oranges. A name
that makes us feel ashamed
though when I see them in my head
that's the word that's there.

*

Three weeks before Christmas
two writers kill themselves.
                First a woman, then a man.
With him it is what he left
that matters: two kids
                a pregnant wife.
With her it is the act itself
that won't let go.

Always when we saw her at a dance
she wore ballet slippers.
We smiled at that.
                Now we wonder
if she slipped her narrow feet
into satin, knotted long pink ribbons

before she tied that other knot,
        her toes perfectly *au point*
spinning small tight circles
above the porcelain tub.

*

Walking to the 7-Eleven at night
for milk and bread. No one else about.
The snow crunches under my boots
like small bones. In the streetlights
the sky is crystal. Each snowflake
lighting on my skin,
            disappears,
sinks through. Tonight as I walk
I am full of stars.

*

We buy a blue spruce, flat
as two hands pressed together.
When it thaws, unfolds its branches
in the dry heat of the house,
the needles fall. I think of
the pregnant woman, her children,
their Christmas tree, the delicate
heirlooms of glass. They break
so easily in her hands.
I remember as a child
the angel hair that went on last,

how beautiful it was,
how it cut my fingers.
Sometimes its long white strands
wore spots of blood.

*

Last year too little money
to fly anywhere, too cold to drive.
We stayed here, shared our turkey dinner
with Luis from Nicaragua, Oscar from El Salvadore.
Only seventeen, Oscar drank Pepsi, practised English:
How do you say . . . , how do you say . . . ?
A teacher in his country, here
Luis shovelled snow. His job would end soon.
Oscar had two more months of English classes.
All night he said, *I speak only*
present tense.

*

I wrap presents,
                  seal them
with bell and blossom stickers.
How I would like to put love inside,
a blessing, a lock of angel hair,
the real thing.
                  A satin ribbon,
the knots pressed out. An orange
whose peel comes off whole.

No broken bits of anything,
no lost pieces.

*

Under the feeder
               bird tracks,
a beautiful cuneiform,
blue shadows in snow.

Maybe sparrows traced the first letters,
our ancestors finding meaning
in the delicate tracks, frail
shapes linked to the things
they saw:
               birds, animals,
               death in winter.

Perhaps the message sparrows leave
makes sense of things,
gives us
        a broken song
to make it through
this long December,
three more months of cold.

*   *   *

THE INFLUENCE
OF AN AVID FISHERMAN
ON ORDINARY LIFE

THE INFLUENCE OF AN AVID FISHERMAN
ON ORDINARY LIFE

(for David)

The fisherman casts on the lawn
and reels in. The grass is wet,
most of the houses still asleep,
the sky clean
                     as washing on the line.
You want to laugh, you want to shout
Hey, you won't catch any fish here!
but there's something you admire
– the gestures repeated
                     just to get it right
as if the fish deserve an equal grace
from this being whose elements
are earth and air.

                     With a sweep of his arm,
he makes the whole neighbourhood
a harbour at dawn.
                     Everything moves
with the moving line. The houses
bob up and down
                     straining at their ropes.
You lick your lips and they taste of salt.
When you whistle, your dog,
sleek and black and webbed between the toes,

dolphins
        off the steps –
and your small, stuccoed house

                        heads for the open

without you.

MOTHER AND I, WALKING

Father is gone again,
the streets empty.
Everyone is inside,
listening to radios
in the warm glow of their stoves.

The cold cries under our boots.
We wade through wind. It pushes
snow under my scarf and collar,
up the sleeves of my jacket.

Mother opens her old muskrat coat,
pulls me inside.
Her scent wraps around me.
The back of my head presses
into the warm rise of her belly.

When I lower my eyes, I see
our feet, mine between hers,
the tracks of one animal
crossing the open,
strange and nocturnal,
moving towards home.

WATCHING THE WHALES

The two Belugas move
through each other's slipstreams,
slide over and around, inseparable
as sound from water.

As they swim out of darkness
they remind her
                    of flesh on flesh,
what she saw through her parents' door,
the pale animal they become
when she's not there.

Now they are watching the whales.
Underground
the only light is from the tank.
Aqua and silver
it moves with the water,
it dapples her skin.

She hears her father say
one of the Belugas is dying of cancer,
its cells gone bad. From the outside
they both look the same.
One stops, stares through the glass
where she is standing.
In its eye, she sees her face,
her red dress – then
it slips away.

When she can't see them
she hears their singing,
so beautiful she can't hold it
in her mind.
        Bel-ooo-ga Bel-oo-ga

Is it loneliness or love,
this sound they're making?

She is watching the whales,
wondering which one is dying,
which one holds her,
her face imprinted
in the cells of its brain.

Years later it will surface
coming white and silent out of dreams toward her.
Already she is crying, hands pressed
against the glass and she won't
come away.

SPIDER

The spider in the heart
of the rose
is a ventriloquist.

It sings on the rose's tongue.
A bee changes direction,
moves its dusty thighs
toward the garden.
The spider says *Sweet release.*

It moves the rose's lips and whispers
to the little moths,
lunar and *lantern light.*

In the circles of its web
it inscribes
the eight names of night.
The rose's silken voice
reads them to the flies,
each word growing softer
so they'll come near.

Inside the heart
the spider sings,
its clever mouth
perfectly still.

HOW BEAUTIFUL THY FEET IN SHOES

(for Roy d. 1987)

1

In his brand new shoes,
fine Italian leather,
soft as chamois on the skin,
           he walked his slow gait,
arms and legs
awkward and stiff,
only the feet
           moving with grace
as if his shoes
had a will of their own.

2

When parts of the body go,
concentrate on what is left.

The feet are beautiful
           when the bones show through.

3

It is his shoes
I want to remember
like the one I saw
in the open grave in Santiago.
A woman's shoe, a black high heel,
an open toe.

I imagine the woman
kicking it off
in a rush to go somewhere,
to dance in her bare feet,
to love
        one more time
with her whole body.

As I want to believe he did
before his cells
                divided him
into too many parts
to live in.

4

The shoes
held the narrow bones
of his feet together
as he walked each morning
down the block and back,
                    letting go of life

as a baby lets its hands
fall from the furniture
                    and almost runs
into that huge space,
the white soles
                    touching ground
the first time.

5

The shoes took him there
as if they'd known all along
where he had to go –
one foot following the other,
the simplest movement,
whether he was walking
toward love or death,
                    his feet moving
from one place
                    to the next.

6

Side by side
          (still warm)
under the bed
          his shoes,
toes in darkness,
heels rounding
                    the light.

No olive trees, no birds
to bless the air. We're above
the shepherds and their goats,
the little huts where fires are built.
It's like driving through God's head,
Patrick says. These sheer cliffs,
this absence of forgiveness.
One more time we're leaving,
starting again in another place.
Not speaking we climb
the cold indifferent air. Only
Patrick's hands on the wheel,
only what we feel for one another
holds us there, the sky breaking
three thousand feet below.
From behind God's eyes, everything's
so glacial, sharp and clear.
From here, there's nowhere else to go.

LINES FOR THE EARTH

A long line of black ants
moves across the sand, so many
they carve a trail. So many
if you step on one, the line
will not break. It is time
tracking itself. It is one
vast mind moving forward.

Ant after ant, each bears
an egg, a round white syllable.
Somewhere they are stringing them
together. Somewhere under the earth
they are spelling it out.

AFTERWORDS

A man is nothing.
A snake even less.
They put a hollow tube
like a drinking straw
between his lips.
In this, they force a snake,
stuff the opening with cloth
soaked in gasoline,
set the cloth on fire.
The snake explodes
down the man's windpipe.
It goes crazy in his lungs,
the man goes crazy.

A snake is not a life,
a woman even less.
Inside a woman
they sew a rat.

You ask me about Chile.
This is why it's so hard
to tell you.

There are sounds
we don't want to know
the meaning of   animals
that live inside us.

I must learn their language –
words to calm a snake
churning in my lungs,
words to make a rat
lie still.

IN PRAISE OF WOMEN

It is not only the women we know,
our friends and sisters, our mothers
climbing the stairs after work,
weariness heavy on their backs. It is also
the women of Greenham Common, their chain
of endurance and belief stretching the heart.
The women of El Salvador, of Nicaragua,
keening for sons and husbands, the lost
villages, the empty places where nothing grows.
The women of Argentina, searching for grandchildren
through the dark pages of their history. The women
of Chile, carrying the faces of the *desaparecidos*
past the soldiers to the gates of torture,
to the cemetery, *NN* painted on the graves.
The women who walk with stones in their hands,
with numbers on their wrists, with pieces of their
bodies missing. The women, blinded with hoods,
raped and beaten in secret rooms across America.
Though they have been broken, they hold babies,
load guns, wash the bodies of the dead. Across borders,
across oceans and the endless reach of prairie,
our sisters, our mothers, our daughters
join hands. These women
make us holy.

A HOUSE TO LIVE IN

Someone walks out a door
that opens on a word.
The word is *you.*

When I say a name
it is yours
and now I can't imagine
life without you.

From your smell,
your touch, the taste
of your skin

I build a house
to live in
all the doors
swinging wide.

HOW TO STOP MISSING YOUR FRIEND WHO DIED

The moon over Vancouver Harbour
is full and red.
Through the window
you can see a barge go by.
It is empty, returning
to whatever country sent it out.

You can't see any lights
but someone must be steering,
someone who doesn't know
you are sitting behind a window
that overlooks the sea.
The moonlight makes the barge
more important than it really is.

Then there's a sailboat
and a heron.
Its legs stretch so far behind
when it's flying
it forgets they're there.

ICARUS IN THE SEA

ICARUS IN THE SEA

" . . . the sun shone
As it had to on the white legs disappearing into the green
Water; and the expensive delicate ship that must have seen
Something amazing, a boy falling out of the sky,
Had somewhere to get to and sailed calmly on."

1

Icarus in the sea
has three hooks
caught
in his upper lip.

He never could
resist a lure
especially the sun's
mad dance
on wings and water,
quicksilver words
that catch the tongue.

2

He is the one
the nets are lowered for

>   net of eyes
>   net of ears

beautiful Icarus
who knows all the elements

    net of mouth
    net of hair
    net of hands

Only breath will hold him
and it is full
of holes.

3

A lot has happened
since Icarus went under.
How he would have loved
the drawings of Leonardo,
Rilke's angels, Boticelli's
Venus rising from the sea,
ethereal Nijinsky
starving his body
into spirit and air.

4

Sometimes Icarus forgets
what world he's in.
The shore erases itself,
draws its line higher
on the sand. The sea

reels in streets and houses,
entire cities
sink into memory, trees
reach out and touch him.
He climbs one
as he did as a boy,
scrapes his shins on the bark.
Less joy in it now,
no fear of falling
                    just a floating away...

5

There are wild horses
                    and limitless space.
Is it enough?
Stars that walk on tiny feet,
rainbows with fins and open mouths,
saws that slice the dark.
Is it enough?

Wolf eels, preying mantas,
gills and lungs, fish
within fish within fish.

Everything imaginable
on earth lives here,
except it is brighter,
more deadly, more ambulant,
alone.

6

One day a house drifts out to sea
like a ship with its lights on.
Icarus opens a door, steps inside.
So little room, so many objects
he doesn't know the meaning of.

He touches a white curtain,
takes a glass from the cupboard,
runs his finger around the rim,
remembers *thirst*.

At the top of the stairs
a Brueghel hangs
in an empty room, the gods
still sending messages
though Icarus will not leave the kitchen.

He is sitting at the table
with his head in his hands.
It is not the two plates
set for the evening meal
that make him weep.
It is the bird painted
on the salt and pepper shakers.

Though he heard it every morning
in his other life,
he can't remember
what sound it makes.

Koo koo koo he cries
Karreep Karree Karroo
putting his fingers to his lips
as if he is learning to speak again
from touch.

7

Is Icarus the golden eagle
that will not drop
the fish
that drags him under?

Or the silver fish –
an eagle's bones
riding his back,
talons hooked
in the soft flesh?

8

Icarus believes
he is in a labyrinth
built by his father,
a watery maze intricate
as a snail's spiral.

He can almost see
the grey head of Daedalus
bent over papers,

the clever fingers drawing
lines from the deepest
part of himself,
twists and turns
flowing into one another,
no beginning, no end.

This is better than thinking
where he is
has no shape or reason.

When he finds the centre,
he knows his father will be there,
unwinding a ball
of clear blue thread.

9

Clouds float
on the surface
Icarus arches
              minus wings and arms

blue dolphin flying
all belly and tail
smack!
        and leap again
smack!

10

No one thinks of him anymore.
The sky will not carry
his messages or the sea.
That ploughman and shepherd
who watched the boy with wings
and thought he was a god
are dead. The maiden who wept for him,
dead. The old fox Daedalus, dead.

Clouds are not enigmas anymore.
They are full of engines and exhaust.
Birds fly into machines,
                              split like atoms.

Close your eyes, Icarus,
try to sleep.
You're too full of longing
for our new mythologies.
You could drown us
in your sorrow.

11

What can console dear Icarus?
The soft noses of dolphins,
the dance of ghost crabs,
the sea-snail that always looks
as though it's going somewhere else.

Everything is outside him.
Even his soul, a moon
jellyfish full of light,
rises and falls
with the whim of the waves,
then drifts away.

12

A high pure sound
(he doesn't know if he is dreaming
or awake)
fills him with such longing
he swims to its source. There
a man in a boat plays a flute –
melodies like terns

                      dipping and soaring

above the waves
light dancing
and air, air, air!

Orpheus, lead me from this dark!

The words come out
in shrieks and moans, shrill whistles,
graceless mime of a song
void of meaning

                  even to the huge
intelligence of the whale.

13

Add up his losses:
the creak of leather on cobblestones,
goat's milk and olives,
steam rising from bread
the knife slices through.
His shadow
that used to walk
ahead or behind
depending on its mood
and the time of day.
The time of day.

He is no longer a boy
but what is he then?

A broken bird, a dream
someone had of flying,
a fish swimming in a wingbone cage?

He is both fish and cage,
both water and what the water sees—
faces of the drowned (their tongues
are stones in their mouths)
and the thin
brittle bones of dream.

14

As the words slip away from you,
Icarus, as the earth did and the sun,
we will not send Rilke's angels,
Boticelli's Venus to comfort you.

Instead a message
                    from mad Nijinsky
who followed your fiery path
across the sky.

> My little girl is singing:
> *Ah, ah, ah, ah!*
> I do not understand its meaning
> but I feel what she wants to say.
> She wants to say that everything
> – Ah! Ah! –
> is not horror
>   but joy.

15

Eight parts water, two
parts air, the rest
hidden light. Long ago
he shook off heaviness
like boots
caked with mud.

At his best,
when his arms beat the splendid air,
when his body cuts through water
like a shark's black fin
                    he is subliminal
song, indelible word

stroked with a feather
across the throat,
the sleeping eye.

16

It is not true
that no one thinks of him
anymore. He has followed
the rivers back to the little streams,
the fishing holes.

He is what moves under
green shadows in prairie sloughs,
what nests in blue
reflections in mountain lakes.

He is always moving
toward the minnow, the nymph,
the feather fly you cast and cast
again. He is the hole in the net
the fisherman pulls up late at night,
the longing for shore, the woman
waiting at the window.

Icarus of sky and water,
you who know the paths of birds
and spawning fish,
we will think of you
as the one we cannot catch,
the one that keeps us
dreaming, the broken
line, the
Ah!

A NOTE ON THE TEXT

Some of the poems in this book have appeared in the following magazines: *Malahat Review; Descant; Event; Prism International; Waves; Dandelion; NeWest Review; Freelance; Montreal Now; Canadian Literature; Fireweed; Poetry Canada Review; Cross-Canada Writers' Quarterly; Yak; Tickle Ace; Moosehead Review; Prairie Fire; CVII; Whetstone; Zymergy;* and *Border Crossings.* Several have been broadcast on CBC's "Ambience," and included in the anthologies *The New Canadian Poets; The Macmillan Anthology; Ride Off Any Horizon; Dancing Visions;* and *The Lyric Paragraph.* The title "Childhood Landscapes" comes from a poem by Charles Wright. A selection of poems from this book brought together under the title "Angels of Silence" received the first prize for poetry in the CBC Radio Literary Competition for *1987–1988*, and were broadcast on CBC's "State of the Arts." The Chilean poems included here were part of a radio script written with Patrick Lane and broadcast on "State of the Arts," winning the Best Program Award at the National Radio Awards, *1988.* The poem, "Fear of Snakes," won second prize in *Prism International*'s poetry competition.

The author would like to thank Donna Bennett for her fine editing, Bronwen Wallace for her title suggestion, the Saskatchewan Artists'/Writers' Colony Committee for providing an environment conducive to writing and the Canada Council and the Saskatchewan Arts Board for their financial assistance.